VENUS

Super Hot

by Dawn Bluemel Oldfield

Consultant: Karly M. Pitman, PhD
Planetary Science Institute
Tucson, Arizona

New York, New York

Credits
Cover, © NASA; TOC, © NASA; 5, © Carlos Clarivan/SPL; 6–7, © Wikipedia & NASA;
8, © NASA; 9, © NASA/JPL; 10–11, © NASA/JPL; 12, © NASA; 13, © 2007 MPS/DLR–PF/
IDA; 14–15, © ESA; 16, © NASA; 17, © NASA/JPL; 18–19, © ESA, Medialab/SPL;
20–21, © Astrobobo/iStock; 23TL, © ESA; 23TM, © Ivan Tykhyi/Thinkstock; 23TR, © NASA/
Wikipedia; 23BL, © ESA, Medialab/SPL; 23BM, © iStock/Thinkstock; 23BR, © iStock/
Thinkstock.

Publisher: Kenn Goin
Editor: Jessica Rudolph
Creative Director: Spencer Brinker
Design: Debrah Kaiser
Photo Researcher: Michael Win

Library of Congress Cataloging-in-Publication Data

Bluemel Oldfield, Dawn, author.
  Venus : super hot / by Dawn Bluemel Oldfield.
     pages cm. — (Out of this world)
  Includes bibliographical references and index.
  ISBN 978-1-62724-562-3 (library binding) — ISBN 1-62724-562-6 (library binding)
  1. Venus (Planet)—Juvenile literature. I. Title.
  QB621.B58 2015
  523.42—dc23
                                    2014036511

For more information, write to Bearport Publishing Company, Inc., 45 West 21st Street, Suite 3B,
New York, New York 10010. Printed in the United States of America.

10 9 8 7 6 5 4 3 2 1

CONTENTS

What is the hottest planet?

VENUS!

The temperature on Venus is about 864°F (462°C).

Venus is part of Earth's Solar System.

JUPITER

MARS

VENUS

EARTH

MERCURY

SUN

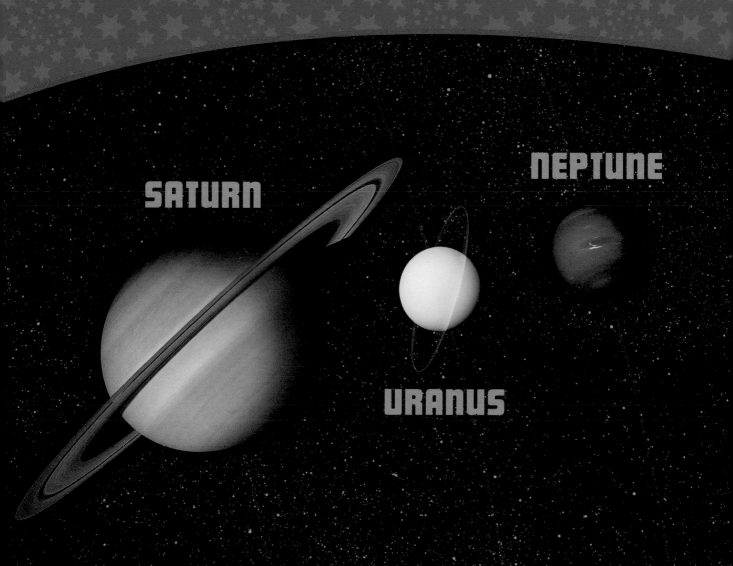

SATURN

NEPTUNE

URANUS

It is the second
planet from the Sun.

Venus is called Earth's twin.

VENUS

EARTH

That's because the two planets are about the same size.

Like Earth, Venus has mountains and valleys.

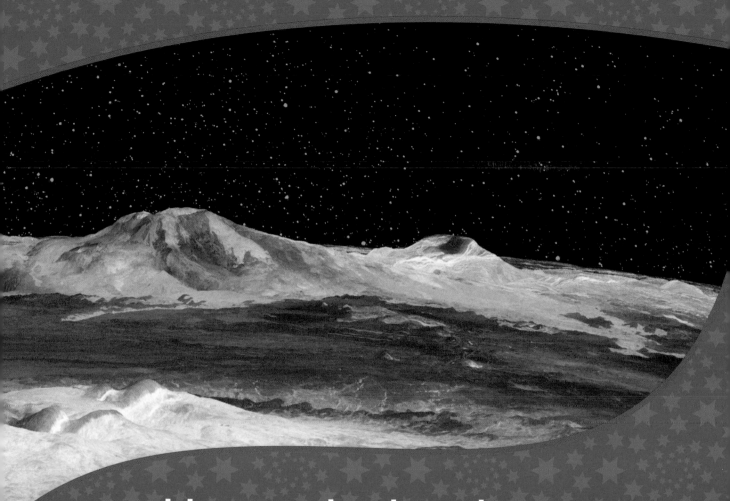

Unlike Earth, the planet
has no oceans. It has no
water on its surface at all!

It never rains on Venus.

However, sometimes
lightning flashes in the sky.

Venus's **atmosphere** is made of **poisonous** gases.

People would die if they breathed in the air.

People have not visited Venus.

However, spacecraft have explored the planet.

They sent information back to Earth.

A spacecraft

moon

VENUS

Sometimes Venus shows up in the night sky.

It's so close, people don't need a telescope to see it.

The bright planet looks like a very large star.

VENUS

VERSUS

EARTH

VENUS	VERSUS	EARTH
Second planet from the Sun	POSITION	Third planet from the Sun
7,521 miles (12,104 km) across	SIZE	7,918 miles (12,743 km) across
About 864°F (462°C)	AVERAGE TEMPERATURE	59°F (15°C)
Zero	NUMBER OF MOONS	One

GLOSSARY

atmosphere (AT-muhss-fihr) gases that surround a planet

poisonous (POI-zuhn-uhss) able to kill or harm a living thing

Solar System (SOH-lur SISS-tuhm) the Sun and everything that circles around it, including the eight planets

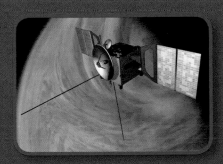

spacecraft (SPAYSS-kraft) vehicles that can travel in space

telescope (TEL-uh-skohp) an instrument that makes faraway objects seem larger and closer

volcanoes (vol-KAY-nohz) mountains or hills that have openings from which hot, liquid rock can shoot out onto the surface of a planet

INDEX

READ MORE

Howard, Fran. *Venus (Planets)*. Edina, MN: ABDO (2008).

Lawrence, Ellen. *Venus: The Hot and Toxic Planet (Zoom Into Space)*. New York: Ruby Tuesday Books (2014).

LEARN MORE ONLINE

To learn more about Venus, visit
www.bearportpublishing.com/OutOfThisWorld

ABOUT THE AUTHOR

Dawn Bluemel Oldfield is a writer. She enjoys reading, traveling, and gardening. She and her husband live in Texas, where they sometimes see Venus in the night sky.